Jaipur

First published 2000

Published by Crest Publishing House
G2, 16 Ansari Road, Darya Ganj,
New Delhi 110002
Ph: (011) 3252366, 3264748 Fax: (011) 3278469
E-mail: sethidel@ndf.vsnl.net.in

Introduction: Gayatri Devi
Edited by: Kishore Singh
Photographs: Gopi Gajwani

Designed by: Yogesh Gajwani and Suraksha Gajwani

ISBN 81-242-0184-6

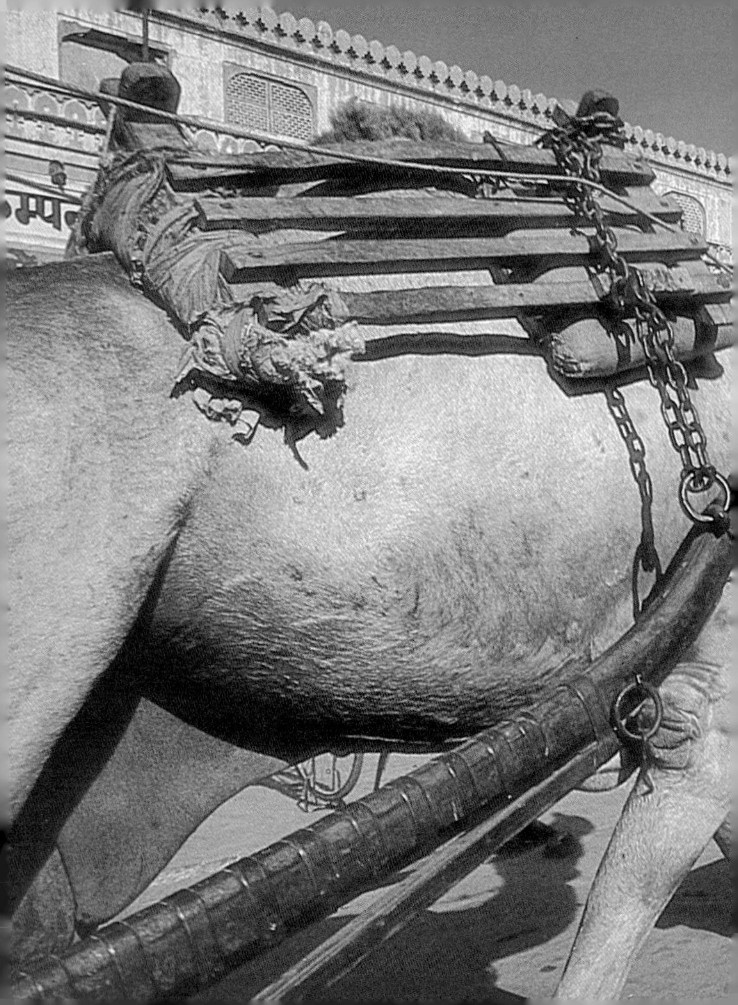

मेटल इन्डस्ट्रीज
बर्फवाला

Jaipur was the capital of the Kachawa kings from 1729 to 1949, its birth and growth inextricably linked with that of its rulers. It is a combination of a splendid creation of architecture, a genius in town planning, and intellectual, cultural, artistic and religious pursuits.

The Kachawas claim direct descent from Kush, the son of the Suryavanshi emperor, Ramchandra, the hero of the epic Ramayana. Much of their early history is chronicled by balladeers, supported by historical evidence and old chronicles. The Kachawas are believed to have first established themselves at Rohtas in Bihar from where they moved to Narwar and Gwalior. It was from there that the Kachawa chieftain, Duleh Rai came to what is now Rajasthan. At Dausa, he married the local chieftain's daughter and laid the foundation of their first capital. There is an interesting incident concerning Duleh Rai who was routed at Manch by the Meenas. Lying wounded, the chieftain had a vision of Goddess Jammuva Mata urging him once more to battle for, she predicted, victory would be his, after which he should lay the foundation of his capital there. As she had prophesied, so it was, and at the spot where he had lain fatigued by the battle still stands a temple dedicated to Jammuva Mata, the family deity of the Jaipur Kachawas.

Duleh Rai named the place Jamwa Ramgarh in thanksgiving to the Goddess and his great forebear, Lord Rama. His son, Kakil Deo subdued the Susawat Meenas, storming their stronghold at Chil-ka Tola where he had a small fort constructed. This was the beginning of Jaipur's Jaigarh Fort. Legend has us believe that the new capital began with the discovery of an auspicious sign of Lord Ambikeshwar (or Shiva) in a tank, and so came to be called Amber.

From 1036 to 1727, Amber remained the Kachawa capital. The new generation of Amber kings continued their territorial expansion and included Raja Man Singh I, a brilliant general and Commander-in-Chief of the Mughal army, and one of the nine gems of Akbar's court. Even while his campaigns took him to distant Kabul, Kandhar and

Bengal, he was able to start building the magnificent palace at Amber. The palace is a perfect specimen of Rajput architecture and his bhojan shala or dining room was decorated later with paintings of the cities of Delhi, Agra, Mathura and other holy places. He had carried the image of Shila Mata from Bengal and had her installed in a small shrine. His architectural genius is evident not only in the palace at Amber but in the remains of the old city beyond the citadel. Among structures that have withstood the ravages of time is the Jagat Shiromani Temple with an image of Girdhar Gopal before which Meerabai would offer her prayers in Chittor; Raja Man Singh had a statue of Meerabai installed next to the deity.

His great grandson, Mirza Raja Jai Singh further embellished the palace in the form of the Ganesh Pol, the beautiful mosaic gate; the Diwan-i-Am, built with red sandstone pillars in the Mughal style; and Jai Mandir, with its square panels of ivory white marble. The Sheesh Mahal is a wonderful example of the mirror-inlay work of the period. From Jas Mandir one gets a view of the hills,

Dilaram-ka-Bagh, Mohan Bari and Maotha Lake. Amber is connected by a steep road to Jaigarh Fort with its spacious and airy palaces. At Jaigarh, during the reign of Mirza Raja Jai Singh, the beautiful palace of Laxmi Vilas, complete with central heating and the royal steam bath, was constructed. Alterations and additions were made during the time of Sawai Jai Singh II and Ram Singh II.

Jaigarh is equally important for another dimension — its gun foundry, built in 1584 by Bhagwan Das and equipped with all the facilities required for casting, drilling and mould making. The Jaivana cannon, constructed here, and still on display, is a medieval wonder. With its barrel 20 feet long, a carriage wheel nine feet high, and weighing 50 tons, it is said to be the largest cannon on wheels in the world. It is because of the legendary treasury and this gun foundry that none but trusted courtiers were allowed entry into Jaigarh Fort.

It was Sawai Jai Singh II who had the fort of Nahargarh constructed in 1734. An interesting incident occurred when this 18th century fort was being built.

Masons found their entire effort of the day destroyed at night, so that they had to begin their labour from scratch everyday. Finally Sawai Jai Singh himself set out to investigate this unusual phenomenon. In the hills he met a *bhomia* called Nahar Singh who told him he lived at the site of the fort and was responsible for its nightly damage. The *bhomia* was given a small fortress in compensation, and Nahargarh was later named after him. Within the fort, the ruler had a well planned and scientifically-laid canal network developed for collecting rain-water to supply the massive tanks of Jaigarh and Nahargarh.

Maharaja Sawai Jai Singh II's most enduring legacy, however, is the city of Jaipur itself. Crowned in 1700 as the ruler of Amber at the young age of 12, he grew into an astute politician and a great general, and was well read and fully deserving of the title of Sawai (one-and-a-quarter) bestowed upon him by Emperor Aurangzeb.

Sawai Jai Singh II found Amber small, and its rocky terrain restricted expansion. It was imperative, therefore, to plan and build a new city where a larger, more prosperous settlement could be established. He chose the open plains at the foot of Nahargarh to build his new capital. He was a proficient astronomer and well versed with Hindu texts, so it is not surprising that his city, though modern in every way, also conformed to the modes of town planning as dictated by the Hindu *shilp-shastras*. Assisting him with his plans was Vidyadhar, a Bengali Brahmin, who was responsible for developing the overall masterplan of the city. His own enchanting garden house is testimony to his impeccable taste.

At noon on Saturday, the 18th of November, 1727, work on the new city began with the foundation laying. Sawai Jai Singh proposed the original plan of the city himself. The town was divided into two linear paths by a road two miles and 40 yards long, running from Suraj Pol in the east to Chand Pol in the west. The rectangular shape of the town was divided into eight blocks (known as *chowkris*), including one block for the palace. The palace block, known as Chowkri Sarhad, Purani Basti and Ramchandraji occupied the road on the north and Topkhana

Hazuri and the road on the south. Five main highways cut each other at right angles to divide the town into uniform squares. The Choti Chaupar and Bari Chaupar squares inside the walled city were embellished with fountains. There were 407 *mohallas* (localities) guarded by seven fortified gateways that used to be closed after 11 pm — a practice that was continued till the reign of Maharaja Sawai Man Singh II. A wall 20 feet high was built around the city, for its location in the plains made it vulnerable.

Jaipur became the first planned city of India. Shops in Johari Bazaar, Sireh Deori Bazaar, Kishanpol Bazaar and Gangori Bazaar were of uniform size and shape. The main street was 111 feet wide. All buildings were made of stone, brick and lime, and positioned in such a way that rooms were well lit without being subjected to the glare of the desert sun.

People were invited to build their houses in areas that were specially reserved for them. There were separate areas for *jagirdars*, prominent citizens, private citizens, merchants, shopkeepers — for those from every strata of society. However, the people could not build as they chose. The height of the building was controlled, and all the plans had to be submitted to Vidyadhar to assure a uniformity in the architectural style of Jaipur. The pattern of the houses was usually the same: a first courtyard followed by a set of rooms and then a courtyard. Even the exteriors of the houses were pleasing with their *jharokas* and trellises.

The central pivot of Sawai Jai Singh's city was the seven-storied Chandra Mahal. The Jai Niwas Garden and the Govind Dev Temple were a part of the complex that consisted of 36 ateliers and 52 administrative departments and, of course, the observatory, better known as Jantar Mantar, with its concrete 'instruments'. Chandra Mahal blended classical Mughal and traditional Rajput architectural styles, and was approached through a series of seven imposing gateways. To its west lay the Zeena Deori with its dozens of halls, temples, *raolas* and mansions for the exclusive use for the royal ladies and their personal staff. The Jai Niwas Bagh, complete with fountains, water channels and reservoirs, was patterned on the Mughal gardens of Kashmir. Today, a part of the palace houses the Maharaja Sawai Man Singh II Museum with the memorabilia of the state on display. Particularly striking are two silver urns that, according to the Guinness Book of Records, are the largest silver objects in the world. The gigantic urns were specially built to carry the Ganga-*jal* required by Maharaja Madho Singh II, who was the first ruler of Jaipur to travel overseas, in the early 20th century. Visitors to the museum can see displays of striking textiles from the royal wardrobe, exquisite carpets, illustrated manuscripts and miniature paintings, and unique armoury and armaments that include swords and daggers with carved heads and inlaid powder boxes.

The Jai Niwas gardens lie behind the Chandra Mahal, from where a fountain flows all the way down to Govind Devji temple, and continues on to the Badal Mahal which overlooks the tank of Talkatora. At one time Badal Mahal must have been a shooting *odhi*. Later it was converted into an atelier for craftsmen of all trades. At that time, one could go by boat all the way from Talkatora to Jal Mahal.

It was fortunate that Sawai Jai Singh's successors continued to enhance Jaipur's beauty, adding to it beautiful buildings, temples and palaces. Ishwari Singh, who lived through troubled times and had to order the city's gate closed against invaders, left behind the beautiful tower, Isar-Lat, known to local dwellers as Swarga Suli, to commemorate his victory against the Marathas. The next ruler, Madho Singh I further enhanced the beauty of the city by adding the Madho Niwas in the Chandra Mahal complex, the Jal Mahal in the centre of the Man Sagar Lake, and the Sisodia Rani ka Bagh.

The Hawa Mahal with its unique architecture has made Jaipur famous throughout the world. It is exquisitely fretted with screens, allowing a play of breezes in the warm summer months. Its screens made it ideal for the women of the royal family to look out on to the streets without themselves being seen. It was built by the poet king Sawai Pratap Singh, who was a great devotee of Radha-Krishna and authored a large number of books under the pen name of Brijnidhi.

His great-grandson, Maharaja Sawai Ram Singh II ascended the throne when only 17 months old. During his long rule as a minor, Jaipur was fraught with intrigues and for the first time British influence appeared to surface in the internal politics of Jaipur. Therefore it is to Maharaja Ram Singh's credit that despite the turmoil and strife that surrounded him during his childhood, he turned out to be one of Jaipur's most enlightened and progressive rulers. He laid the beautiful Ram Niwas Bagh and it was during his time that the streets were paved and the gas-works introduced for street lighting. He was a great patron of arts and started the Maharaja School of Arts and Crafts. He also started the first high school for boys and girls, the first modern hospital, and a theatre in Jaipur. It was during his reign that Prince Albert, the consort of Queen Victoria, visited Jaipur and he is said to have had the city painted pink for the occasion. He commemorated this visit by building a public hall and a public museum in the Ram Niwas Bagh. He was a brilliant photographer, and was also very keen on flying kites. On Makar-Sankranti, when his kite was cut, he sent for the man who had cut his kite and learnt about the use of '*manjha*' from him. He invited the man, a potter, and his community to live in his city and practice their trade, and that is how the blue pottery, for which Jaipur is famous, first came to Jaipur.

He was succeeded by Maharaja Madho Singh II who added several useful public buildings to the city of Ramgarh, and many other dams, for irrigation and water supply.

His successor was Maharaja Sawai Man Singh II, the last ruling king of the Kachawa clan. He was responsible for modernising Jaipur and expanding it beyond the city walls in a well thought out plan, like his forefather Sawai Jai Singh. Educational institutions like the Maharaja College, the Maharani College, SMS Medical College and Hospital and later the Maharani Gayatri Devi School and the Bhagwan Das Barracks (which now house the Rajasthan Government Secretariat) along with the Civil Lines, with spacious bungalows for high officials, were added. He expanded the Rambagh complex into a magnificent palace. He had a great sense of foresight and in order to preserve the artistic and architectural heritage of Jaipur, he converted most parts of the City Palace into a public museum and the Rambagh Palace into a luxurious hotel, both of which are now well known throughout the world.

What makes Jaipur so very special today is difficult to pinpoint, but perhaps it is the happy marriage of the old with the new. Or, perhaps, it is the polite courtesy, the *tameez* of the people. Though a modern city it is still unpolluted, and there is a certain 'freshness' to the air. In spite of its location, on the verge of barren lands and desert, Jaipur was full of green forests and wildlife. Though the jackals and tigers seem to have disappeared, you can still hear partridges call. Peacocks flutter on rooftops, stir across courtyards and fan out their vibrant tail feathers to dance.

Holi is played here with great enthusiasm, but it is at Govind Dev temple, where thousands of citizens collect on the occasion of Phaag, that one can see the real spirit of Jaipur. On the occasion of Sheetla Ashtami, the goddess of small pox is still propitiated and the government's buses run through the day to Sheetla Mata's temple, 17 km from the city. A lot of them also assemble in the Ram Niwas Bagh in the centre of the city. Men wear pink turbans and all citizens of Jaipur eat cold food on that day. In October-November, on the occasion of Sharad Poornima, people wear pale pink and kheer is placed out overnight to catch the moonlight before being eaten the next day.

Jaipur is home to all communities and the people participate enthusiastically in all festivals. During Moharrum, many beautifully decorated *tazias* are taken out in processions through the city to the Jal Mahal, the cremation place for the *tazias*. And, at Atish gate, a beautifully decorated silver and gold *tazia* (donated by the Maharaja of Jaipur to the Waqf) can also be seen in the procession on Moharrum.

Jaipur is also an important place of pilgrimage among Vaishnavites for their principal divinities are located in the temples of Galtaji and Govindji. People from all over India visit these temples and also those of Ganeshji at Moti Doongri and Hanumanji near Chand Pol.

The area between Amber and Nahargarh is full of fascinating buildings. As one passes through the Ghat from

Amber to Jaipur, on the left is a palatial building, a temple dedicated to Radha Mohan. It was here that the image of Govind Devji from Brindavan was first brought by Sawai Jai Singh II before being finally installed in the Jai Niwas Bagh. Further along are Man Sagar and Jal Mahal, and *chattris* and temples with painted ceilings and panels. Still further are mansions that must have once housed noblemen and courtiers. The Yajna Sthal, where Sawai Jai Singh II performed the Ashwamedha Yajna, is also located here. Further along the historic road is Brahmapuri, the peaceful retreat of the Brahmins who served the Kachawas as preceptors, priests and counsellors. And still further is Gaitore where beautiful cenotaphs commemorate the Kachawa lineage from the time of Sawai Jai Singh to Sawai Man Singh II, carved out of marble and dedicated to their indomitable spirit of courage.

Once Jaipur was also famous for its horses. The palace stables or *atish* which contained 170 horses, have now been unfortunately converted into a crowded market-place. Still reminiscent of the past, and standing proud, is a carved stone pavilion from where the 'master of the horses' would direct the exercise of the horses. From the 1930s till the end of the '60s, the name of Jaipur was synonymous with polo. The late Maharaja Sawai Man Singh had a handicap of nine and his team, Jaipur, was almost invincible. Till today, polo matches are well attended and Jaipurians understand and follow the sport with interest.

This is the city that was once famous for its Gunjan Khana, the centre of music and performing arts which gave birth to the Jaipur *gharana* or school of Dhrupad music and Kathak dance. Even now, in the early hours of the morning or in the afternoon, when traffic stills for a moment, music emanates from the City Palace, capturing the magic of Jaipur in that instant.

The motifs that brighten the walls of the fort at Amber combine Rajput love for art with Mughal ornamentation, to create vivid embellishments.

The palace in Jaipur formed the centre of the city that was built by Sawai Jai Singh II when he decided to shift his capital here from Amber, and all its trappings were truly royal.

Ganesh Pol, the beautifully painted entrance to the inner apartments at Amber, represents the Rajput love for art, while invoking the blessings of Ganesh, the elephant-headed god who is a remover of all obstacles.

Left and above: The pavilions and kiosks and cupolas of Amber fascinate visitors today, but must have provided their medieval occupants with a view over the lands they commanded.
Overleaf: the many columned halls of Amber are reminiscent of their Mughal counterparts in Delhi and Agra.

Preceding pages: The ornate entrances to different apartments are decorated with paintings, and have doors in relief. Facing page and above: Different views of Amber, the former capital of the ruling family of Jaipur, with its Rajput and Mughal styles of architecture.

Amber rides the crest of the Aravalli hills, its apartments built to capture the views and the summer breezes, though its lower walls rise sheer and invincible from the gully below.

The ramparts of Amber (these pages and overleaf) are protective flanks that provided the warriors enough room from which to deflect their foes; the ramps and battlements were ideal even for a cavalry charge.

Preceding pages and below: The pierced stone screens of Nahargarh fort overlook the valleys and hills that it crowns. Facing page: An overview of the apartments at Nahargarh with their cusped roofs, so characteristic of the Rajput style.

The apartments within Nahargarh are painted and embellished in the araish style, with arches and painted glass lending them a cool elegance in the heat of the summer months.

Below: The walls of Nahargarh are punctured with open windows.
Bottom: At pavilions like this, formal ceremonies would be enacted.
Facing page: The battlements of Nahargarh nurtured the growth of the city of Jaipur that spreadeagles below.

Preceding pages and above: The fascinating Albert Hall Central Museum in the Ram Niwas Public Gardens has been designed by Sir Swinton Jacob in the Indo-Saracenic style.
Facing page: The façade of Hawa Mahal consists almost entirely of windows of different sizes.

Facing page and left: Facets of the Hawa Mahal which provided the women of the City Palace a glimpse of life in the streets. They would look out while seated in the many corridors and balconies (top) that formed the inner part of this palace.

Sawai Jai Singh II, the founder of the city, was also an avid astronomer, and laid the city's huge observatory complex with instruments crafted using masonry to study and monitor the configuration of the planets.

ॐ

Preceding pages, left and below: The city's architecture is a binding force. No building was allowed unless it had been personally cleared by its architect, Vidyadhar. The uniform ochre colour, however, was a later development.

मोहनलालटाँक
एडवोकेट

Preceding pages, above and right: The architectural style of Jaipur is consistent, a marvel of balconies, windows, railings, arches, pillars, staircases, all of them fitting into one whole.

The people of Jaipur continue to dress in the traditional mode despite its cosmopolitan appeal as the capital of the state.

Facing page and above: Women in their colourful clothes, complete with silver and gold jewellery. Preceding pages: The men wear turbans that are equally vibrant.

A printer uses vats of different colours (above) to achieve the beautiful tie-and-dye prints (facing page) associated with his art, a tradition that is still popular.

The streets of Jaipur are full of people plying their trade from the pavements, selling everything from baskets and vegetables to leather footwear and other items of daily use.

Facing page and above: The vegetable markets and flower sellers pile their products in enticing mounds in the lanes of the walled city.
Overleaf: The bazaars of Jaipur bustle with activity; these shops have existed for almost three hundred years, and specialise in different products.

R.C.SHAH & CO.
सम्पति क्रय विक्रय केन्द्र
फैशन पैलेस
लक्की जनरल स्टोर

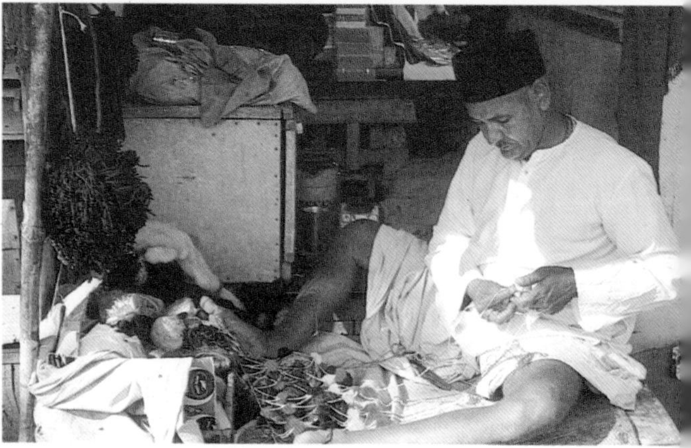

Preceding pages, facing page and above: Pots and pans, beads and threads, kites and quilts, fabrics and dresses –you'll find everything in the shops of Jaipur, one of the world's leading centres for handicrafts.

In Jaipur, there are islands of stillness to be found even amidst the bustle of the bazaar where the people come in any of several modes of transport.

SULZEM

Above: Pierced screen windows capture any hint of breeze, and allow privacy even for houses located just off the streets.
Facing page: Doors feature handles that are both strong as well as ornamental.

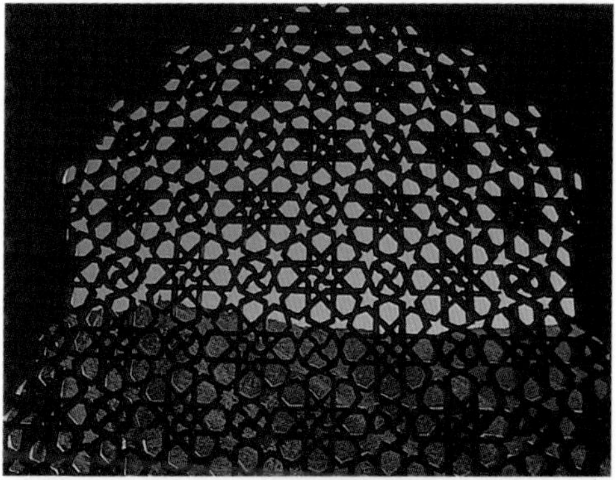

Whether at Amber (preceding pages), the Sheesh Mahal with its mirror inlay (facing page) or the stone work at Nahargarh (above), the architecture of the entire city has a thematic unity that bridges different centuries.

Fresco art was widely prevalent in Rajasthan, and in Jaipur it can be found in the City Palace complex (facing page) as well as Nahargarh (this page). The influence of Mughal miniatures is evident in these works.

This page: Amber overlooks the waters of Maotha lake that offered it its water supply as well as a protective barrier. Facing page: Jaigarh stands above a narrow valley, and was one of the ancient citadels of the Kachawa rulers.

Jal Mahal is an island palace set within the waters of a shallow lake that was once a hunting lodge at the base of Amber. Overleaf: Monkeys scamper over the fortifications of Amber where once soldiers would have kept vigil.

The people's faith lives on in Jaipur, evident in the many roadside shrines, in the images and icons of gods on sale, and in the fortune-teller's performing parrot that discloses what your future has in store for you.